The Religious and Ethical Issues

Fr Brian Lucas

E.J. Dwyer

First published in 1992 by
E.J. Dwyer (Australia) Pty Ltd
3/32-72 Alice Street
Newtown NSW 2042
Australia

National Library of Australia
Cataloguing-in-Publication data

Lucas, Brian Joseph, 1952–
Life at all costs?: the religious and ethical issues.

ISBN 0 85574 093 0.

1. Right to die — Religious aspects — Catholic Church. 2. Right to die — Moral and ethical aspects. 3. Terminal care — Religious aspects — Catholic Church. 4. Terminal care — Moral and ethical aspects. I. Title. (Series: Pocket topics).

241.6424

Typeset in Versailles 11/12pt by Graphicraft, Hong Kong
Printed in Singapore by Kim Hup Lee Printing Co Pte Limited.

"Nihil Obstat: Rev. Kenneth Sargent, D.D.,
Imprimatur: + David Cremin, D.D., V.G.
Date: Sydney, N.S.W. 20.03.92.
The Nihil Obstat and Imprimatur are a declaration that a book or pamphlet is considered to be free from doctrinal or moral error. It is not necessarily implied that those who have granted them agree with the contents, opinions or statements expressed".

Introduction

Modern technology has given medical professionals power to prolong life even in the face of the most extreme life threatening illness.

Intensive care units in hospitals are filled with complex machines that monitor and support those who are at the edge of life and death.

Even when a person's brain has stopped functioning, and the person is described as 'brain dead', technology can maintain a heartbeat and breathing for some time. Advances in transplant surgery now mean that the organs from these patients can be recovered and another sick person given a new chance at life.

When a person is seriously ill the technology provides an opportunity for the body to recover. Sadly, in some cases there is no likelihood of this recovery.

James had been knocked off his motorcycle. He suffered severe brain damage and had been unconscious for weeks. There were no signs of improvement and the life support machines in the intensive care unit were keeping him alive. Gradually his various bodily functions deteriorated. The doctors were satisfied that there was no possibility that he could recover.

At what point should the life support system be withdrawn?

Who can make this decision when the patient is unconscious?

Susan was nearly ninety. She had suffered for about three years with cancer and, in spite of surgery and extensive chemotherapy, her condition had worsened. She was virtually in a coma and the doctors did not expect that she would live for long.

How aggressively should Susan be treated?

Should she be resuscitated and linked up to the life support machines in the intensive care unit if her heart stops beating?

Matthew was born very prematurely. His lungs were not properly developed. He suffers other handicaps and it is likely that if he survives he will be permanently paralysed and not have sight or hearing. There is a fear of brain damage.

What efforts should be made to prolong Matthew's life?

Should he be put on life support systems – or only given palliative care that would make him comfortable until death occurred?

Is the poor 'quality of life' a relevant issue in making these decisions?

Controversy

One of the controversial issues facing society in countries around the world concerns the way we handle these difficult life and death decisions.

When is it right to stop some treatment that does not seem to be of any benefit?

Are doctors obliged to do everything that is possible to preserve life at all costs?

Some groups in the community suggest that when life is nearing its end people should be allowed, even encouraged, to take matters into their own hands and end their lives.

Others go further and would allow doctors or others to assist in this suicide or even take the initiative and, with the patient's consent, end the person's life.

There are organisations which campaign for changes in the law to allow some of these practices.

Others strongly oppose any such suggestions. They hold that life is sacred and may not be prematurely ended, no matter how fragile or distressing such a life may be.

What is the right way of acting? What is best for the patient? What does society expect from its medical professionals?

Every day medical professionals have to make life and death decisions. Every day family and friends are consulted by the professionals and become involved in the decisions about the type of treatment that is suitable for those with life-threatening illness.

Drawing on the tradition of Catholic theology, this booklet will consider some of these questions and explore the religious and ethical issues that arise when decisions have to be made about stopping medical treatment.

Making good moral choices

Those who are responsible for making decisions about what medical treatment is appropriate for a particular patient have to understand the meaning of right and wrong, so that they know what it is they *ought* to do.

This is an *ethical question*. Ethics is the study of moral behaviour. Moral behaviour involves choosing to act in a way that is right and good.

There is a difference between knowing what one *can do* and knowing what one *ought to do*. The fact that some treatment or medical procedure is available does not mean that it ought to be used.

In deciding whether doing or omitting to do an action will be right, we have to take into account two things.

Firstly, there is the likely consequence of the action. Will this action bring about a consequence that is good or bad?

Secondly, as well as looking at the consequences, the intention of the person who is doing the action is important.

Moral decision-making involves taking personal responsibility. We cannot be held to be morally responsible for some action that we did not intend.

A simple example will illustrate this important ethical principle.

Suppose two people, in two separate incidents, knocked over and killed a pedestrian. One was an accident which the driver could not avoid, and the other was an underworld execution. In both cases the consequences of the action of running the person down was the same – the person was killed. In one case there was no intention to kill and in the other there was. The first example did not involve a morally wrong action, the second one obviously did.

A problem with language

Unfortunately, in much of the public debate about these issues, the language that is used is ambiguous.

The word 'euthanasia' is sometimes used

to refer to the action of ending the life of someone who is thought to be 'terminally ill'.

[Even the expression 'terminal illness' is ambiguous. It also has the unfortunate connotation that the person with such an illness is no longer worth caring for. For this reason the expression — 'life-threatening illness' is preferred.]

Sometimes people speak of active euthanasia and passive euthanasia. They presume that active euthanasia means doing something positive to end a person's life while passive euthanasia means withdrawing a treatment. This type of distinction is inaccurate and misleading.

If fact we have to distinguish three possibilities.

Firstly, one can do something positive intending to take a person's life (giving an overdose of medication).

Secondly, one can deliberately omit to do something intending, by that omission, to take a person's life (not providing necessary life-supporting medication).

Both of these actions are immoral and

could rightly be called respectively active and passive euthanasia.

The third possibility involves doing something (administering pain relief) or not doing something, (continuing artificial life support) which may result in the person's death but without any intention to bring about death.

The intention is either to relieve pain, or cease some treatment that is judged to be futile.

This important distinction will be very relevant later on in this booklet when we consider some of the problems that confront medical professionals who have to decide about withdrawing treatment.

In summary, therefore:

We act immorally when we do what we ought not to do, or do not do what we ought to do. What we ought to do or not do will be determined by taking into account whether the consequences of the action are good or bad, as well as the intention behind the action or omission.

Good and Evil

In trying to work out what moral choice will be a good one, we have to have some idea of what 'good' and 'evil' mean.

Not only medical professionals, but patients and relatives have to come to terms with their own attitudes and values and what they mean by good and evil.

Doing what is right, or making a good moral choice will depend on one's vision of the human person, as well as attitudes to the meaning of human suffering, the meaning of 'quality of life' and acceptance of the reality of death.

Some people see no value at all in sickness and suffering, while others see the opportunities that suffering presents for people to come closer to those they love and care about.

We have to recognise our values and identify what we consider to be good and evil.

For some people these values and attitudes are determined by their religious faith.

While good moral choices do not necessarily depend on religious faith, it may be that the religious perspective which a person has on life can help resolve some of the hard decisions which must be made from time to time.

Belief in God can help some people work out what good and evil mean.

No ventilators in the Bible!

Christianity is what is called a revealed religion. There is a belief that God has entered into relationship with, or communicated with, humankind.

While the Bible provides many people with a code of moral conduct, it does not answer all the ethical questions that modern medicine provokes. There is nothing in the Bible about ventilators or intensive care units or proper dosages for pain relief.

The answers to the ethical questions, and even the way the questions are asked, will depend, to some extent, on the vision that we have of humankind. Here theology has something to say about values and the meaning of good and evil.

In determining what is right or wrong we will be guided by our values. It is always good to reflect on the way in which choices are determined by priorities and values.

We need to think through what we understand by suffering. We have to recognise the subjective nature of suffering. While physical pain is, at least to some extent, objectively determined, the capacity of individuals to endure pain can be quite subjective. An inconvenience or frustration for one person becomes burdensome suffering for another.

We must be careful not to impose on others our perception of what is a meaningful life or a suitable quality of life.

An elderly, arthritic lady recently parachuted from a plane at 3,000 metres for the first time in her life. She found the whole experience elating! Her one wish is to jump from even higher up next time! For another woman of her age and condition, that same experience could have been the most terrifying thing that ever happened to her. We all have very different views about 'quality of life'.

Only human

We can wish forever that life had treated us differently but all human beings have limitations. Some are plagued by sickness and ask, 'Why me?' Others cope with their disabilities. Some face death with peace and serenity, while others are anxious and disturbed.

How do we make sense of life's great disappointments – the discovery that we are only a human being?

Even life that appears to be barely worth living to the detached and 'objective' observer may well be acceptable to the person whose only life it is. That person might say – 'this life may not be much but it's all I've got'.

At the very heart of medical ethics, therefore, is the decision about the value of the human person.

Unique!

We find in the Book of Genesis (Gen. 1:27) the claim that God created humankind in the image of himself.

The human person is unique in all creation. That uniqueness is expressed most obviously in the capacity of the human person for self-conscious reflection, communication and, most importantly, in the capacity for personal intimacy.

This ability to love others provides the basis for what is called self-transcendence. This means that the human person is able to direct his or her attention to other people or other values that go beyond mere self-interest and personal survival.

Self-transcendence will be the basis for decisions about life and death and the care that we owe to fellow human beings. It forms the basis for such virtues as justice and charity, which control and guide morally worthwhile human relationships.

One of the most beautiful scenes in the Gospels, relevant to the problems of death and dying, is the visit by Jesus to the tomb of his friend Lazarus. The shortest verse in all the Bible, two words, says, 'Jesus wept' (Jn 11:35). The people said, 'See how much he loved him' (Jn 11:36). The sadness of death, the tears, the grief we experience – this is the price we pay for having had the opportunity to love and care. It is what makes us truly human.

Where God comes in

When we reflect on the possibility of a relationship between God as creator and human being as creature, we discover the limits of personal autonomy and self-determination.

If one accepts that one's life is from God, and for God, then it is God who has final control over life.

We cannot deliberately end the life of an innocent person without violating the unique love relationship between God and that person. We cannot despairingly end our own lives without repudiating that relationship with God.

Even those who do not believe in God can arrive at similar conclusions. If we accept a general moral principle that we should treat others as we would want them to treat us, we can appreciate how important it is to respect the lives of others and why it is immoral to deliberately end the life of an innocent human being.

The decisions about treating or not

treating those suffering a life-threatening illness are not made simply at an intellectual level. We cannot ignore the feelings and emotions.

We may know at the intellectual level that in a particular case terminating treatment is the right decision. Yet some people may still be uncomfortable with implementing the decision because of fears and anxiety about death.

A very personal matter

The process of dying is very personal and very complex. People approach death with a variety of reactions, from outright denial to warm acceptance.

What helps most people face the inevitability of death is the capacity to be detached from the things that no longer matter.

> *What is most valuable when there is only a short time to go is not so much the size of the bank balance, but whether a loved one is there to hold your hand.*

'People whose highest values are transcendent rather than materialistic will be likely to face death more peacefully.

For many people belief in life after death can help. The experience of death holds less threat if, as the Catholic funeral liturgy says, *'the sadness of death gives way to the bright promise of immortality'.*

It is important to meditate on the reality of death at some length because the attitude we bring to the reality that every person we know will one day be dead, will affect ethical decisions to terminate treatment when death has come or when, in the face of inevitable death, treatment is now futile.

Still living, though dying

'Death with dignity' is a commonly used expression but it is not always properly understood. A better way of speaking is to refer to 'living with dignity', even to the moment of death. *Even while dying, a person is still living.*

Dignity refers to human worth.

We devalue a human person when we regard the person simply as a functionary or as an object. We demean human dignity when we use people as means to an end.

Making right moral choices about

treatment means acting in a way that will promote human dignity.

The choices that must be made about treatment take place within the context of the relationship between a person as patient and the medical professional, a relationship that is built on mutual respect and trust. Human relationships are central to the meaning of human worth and human dignity.

It is a denial of human worth, and a breaking of mutual respect and trust, to demand that a person take part in an immoral taking of life.

On the other hand we do not treat a person with respect and promote their dignity if futile or excessively burdensome treatments are imposed against another's will.

Sally had spent most of the last six months in hospital. She appreciated the efforts that the doctors were making but she knew that she was now in the final stages of her disease. Death was inevitable and she accepted that. She wanted to go home and be with her family. She told the doctors not to try any more.

Patients have a right to autonomy. They are entitled to make their own decisions about the treatments that they consider to be appropriate. When inevitable death is imminent, they can refuse treatments that will only secure a precarious and burdensome prolongation of life.

This right is not absolute. It is qualified by the moral obligation to take *reasonable* steps to preserve and protect one's life. One cannot commit suicide by refusing to undergo reasonable lifesaving treatments. To do this is to deny one's own dignity and worth.

Modern problems

When can we cease intensive care therapy, or, to use the unfortunate but popular expression, 'switch off the machine'?

When can we decide not to provide any more treatment to a patient with an advanced and incurable cancer?

Is it right to resuscitate a patient when

death from a life-threatening illness is inevitable and imminent?
How aggressively does one treat a premature newborn who has multiple handicaps and is not likely to survive in spite of the treatment?

These practical questions arise today because of our modern technology. In the past most of the patients who are saved by modern technology would have quickly died.

In the past, however, the same questions did arise, but they dealt with different medical problems. What we find, therefore, is a consideration of similar general principles.

Alphonsus de Liguori (d.1787) was one of the great moral theologians. A civil lawyer as well, he brought a practical wisdom to his moral theology. In his teaching on the duty to preserve life he made these four points:

1) There is no obligation to use costly or uncommon medicines;
2) One need not move to a more heathful climate;

3) One is not required to use difficult or extraordinary means of preserving life, such as the amputation of a leg; and
4) One might have an obligation to use ordinary medication if there was a good hope of recovery.

The examples reflected the state of medicine at the time. Having a leg amputated at a time before anaesthesia and convenient prosthetics would have been quite extraordinary treatment although it is commonplace today.

Ordinary or extraordinary

The distinction used to be made between ordinary treatment, which was morally obligatory, and extraordinary treatment, which was not.

This distinction was made in a famous address given on 24th November, 1957 by Pope Pius XII to an international congress of anaesthesiologists. It was often quoted in textbooks on medical ethics.

This terminology is not so useful today. Rapid changes in technology mean that what was once extraordinary is now quite ordinary.

A new formula had to be devised to express the limits that were to be placed on the obligation to have recourse to particular treatments.

A document was produced in 1980 by the Vatican's Sacred Congregation for the Doctrine of the Faith. The document was entitled *Declaration on Euthanasia**. It accepted the proposition that a patient did not have to undergo every possible remedy that might be available. It then introduced the idea of proportion between the benefits of the teatment and burdens that the patient would have to endure.

Some practical guidelines

1. There is no moral obligation on anyone to undertake medical treatments that are excessively burdensome, costly, risky, or intrusive, taking into account the likely benefit. This benefit is measured in terms of the likely suc-

---

* 'Everyone has the duty to care for his or her own health or to seek such care from others. Those whose task it is to care for the sick must do so conscientiously and

cess of the treatment in the light of what it is meant to do, not value judgments about the quality of another person's life.

---

administer the remedies that seem necessary or useful. However, is it necessary in all circumstances to have recourse to all remedies?

'In the past moralists replied that one is never obliged to use "extraordinary" means. This reply, which in principle still holds good, is perhaps less clear today, by reason of the imprecision of the term and the rapid progress made in the treatment of sickness.

'Thus some people prefer to speak of "proportionate" and "disproportionate" means. In any case, it will be possible to make the correct judgment as to the means by studying the type of treatment to be used, its degree of complexity or risk, its cost and the possibilities of using it, and comparing those elements with the result that can be expected, taking into account the state of the sick person and his or her physical and moral resources.

'When inevitable death is imminent, in spite of the means used, it is permitted in conscience to take the decision to refuse forms of treatment that would only secure a precarious and burdensome prolongation of life, so long as the normal care due to the sick person in similar cases is not interrupted. In such cases the doctor has no reason to reproach himself with failing to help the person in danger.'

Suggested Reading:

Sacred Congregation for the Doctrine of the Faith, *Declaration on Euthanasia*, Vatican City, 1980.

2. There is no moral obligation to attempt the impossible, or undertake treatments that are futile.

3. Patients are entitled to make their own judgments about the treatment they consider to be appropriate. They have the moral responsibility to inform themselves about the treatment, its risks and likely outcome.

4. Patients cannot refuse to undertake reasonable treatments, for to do so is to fail in one's duty to take care of one's health and life.

5. Medical professionals have no right to impose treatments against a patient's will, for to do so is to treat the patient as an object and not as a person.

6. When the patient is not competent, decisions about treatment may be made by the person authorised, either by private arrangement or the authority of law, to speak on that person's behalf.

7. A personal representative has the obligation to promote the best interests of the patient and attempt as far as possible to implement the patient's rightful wishes.

Useless treatment

It seems obvious to say there is no moral obligation to do what is impossible or what is futile. However, in the everyday world of high technology medicine, it is natural that those who are trying to save a life will be tempted to try every treatment that is available. One must admire this commitment and zeal, while recognising that there are limits to what can sometimes be done.

If we concentrate on that simple proposition that there is no moral obligation to attempt the impossible, we can resolve many of the problems that arise in medical practice.

When one can say in truth and love that there is nothing more that can be done that is reasonably likely to bring about the recovery of the patient, the withdrawal of the useless treatment is morally permitted. One cannot expect any more from the medical profession.

In everyday practice, decisions about appropriate treatments are complex because various values must be weighed.

We have to be concerned about the prognosis, the wishes of the patient if these are known, the cost and availability of treatments in the broader social context, and the burden of the treatment for this particular patient. All of this must centre on the real case and the fact that there is a real person in the bed.

It is often dangerous to try to talk about hypothetical cases and try to give hard and fast answers that are only theoretical.

Applying these principles requires, most of all, a good understanding of this particular patient's medical condition. Before one makes decisions about what is ethical one has to know what treatments are available, the medical history, what the likely outcomes will be, and what possibilities face the patient.

Good medical information is indispensable to making good ethical decisions.

What about the law?

As well there are social concerns, and the laws of all societies deal with the attitude we take to human life.

There are some people who claim that the law prohibits withdrawal of useless treatment and they claim that if such withdrawal leads to the death of the patient, then there may be legal liability for damages or even the risk of being charged with a criminal offence.

Intention is relevant to the determination of whether an action is right or wrong morally (this was explained above with the example of the pedestrian deaths) and usually it is relevant in the determination of criminal responsibility.

One can intend to take a person's life and achieve this by withdrawing a life support machine. This would be immoral.

However, if it is reasonably clear that the life support machine is no longer useful in giving the person a chance to recover, then the decision to cease the treatment involves a different intention. The intention is not to kill the patient, although death may be foreseen. The intention is to stop doing something that is no longer of any use.

While it is true that the outcome or consequence may be the same – the patient's death – the intention is different and so the moral quality of the action is different.

Another way of understanding this problem is to realise that when a useless treatment is withdrawn, it is not the withdrawing of the treatment that kills the patient but the underlying illness.

In other cases an action may have two outcomes. Both may be foreseen but only one is intended. For example a patient may be given medication to relieve pain. One outcome is that the pain is controlled, the other outcome is that the patient's life might be shortened as the result of the use of the drugs.

If one intends to kill the patient by the dosage of medication, this would be immoral. If one only intends to relieve the pain and the dosage is no more than is necessary to achieve that result then the action will be moral, even if one of the unintended consequences is that the patient's life is somewhat shortened.

One must always distinguish cases where the treatment was withdrawn as a way of ending the person's life, from cases where it was withdrawn because it was futile or disproportionately burdensome.

Medical personnel are human beings. The decisions of doctors and nurses and the relatives with whom they may consult are human decisions. As human beings we have limited knowledge, wisdom and prudence. Decision-makers are only obliged to do their best in the light of the particular circumstances.

The fear or hesitancy about withdrawing a useless treatment may result from a denial of death or a feeling of failure, or it may be the product of a fear of being sued. The result is that treatments that are useless may be unduly prolonged, causing unnecessary distress to patients.

When we do our best, imperfect though that might be, we have done what has been demanded of us in our care for those we love.

Some people do not think that the law has any role to play in medical decisions. This is not the case. It is possible that decisions could be made about withdrawing treatment so that people's lives are wrongly brought to an end. The law is necessary to protect people from such wrongdoing.

The law is necessary but it must be carefully formulated so that it reflects the ethical principles that have been described above.

The law is important if we are to resist social pressures that would seek to undermine human rights and devalue life.

Telling the truth with love

Communication between doctors, nursing staff, patients where this is possible, and relatives, is most important.

We deny human worth and dignity if we make decisions for other people and do not respect their autonomy.

When people understand what is involved and feel part of the process of decision-making, outcomes are usually more satisfactory. How often do we hear the complaint, *'What I objected to was not so much what was done but the way it was done'*.

We have to be particularly sensitive to relatives who are trying to cope with the fact that their loved one is suffering a life-threatening illness.

One commentator who wrote about euthanasia claimed that most of the pressure for ending a sick person's life came from the relatives who were not coping with seeing their loved one so sick. The relatives were saying, in effect, 'We want to put the patient out of *our* misery'.

Good palliative care involves a team effort that will reassure patients, control their symptoms, take away their fears and provide support for those who are close to them.

When we are committed to the truth and to communicating the truth in love (to paraphrase St. Paul's Letter to the Ephesians 4:15) we demonstrate our love for the patient and the patient's relatives. People will have confidence in the decision.

There will be trust and peace when care is taken to tell the truth with love.

The truth, by itself, can often hurt. We must be aware of how we tell the truth. It is important for medical professionals to give people time, support them in their grief, and give them love.

We will never work out in advance every answer to every likely problem. We do our best. God asks no more.